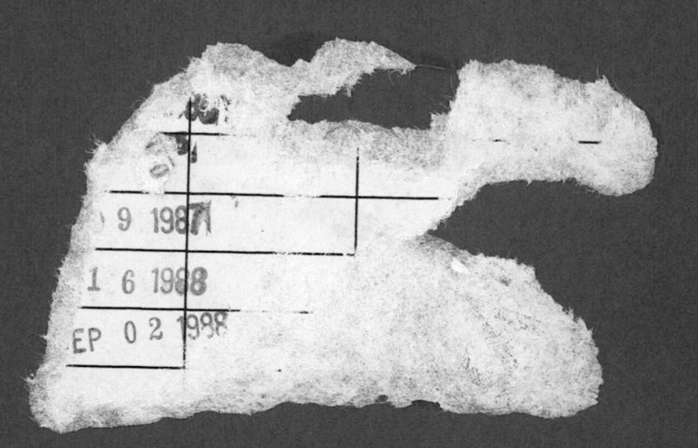

DATE DUE

THE MORRIS APPROACH

Books by Barbara Burn

The Morris Approach: An Insider's Guide to Cat Care
The Horseless Rider

Books Co-Authored by Barbara Burn

Mutt (with Nancy Dolensek)
The Whole Horse Catalog (with Steven Price)
The Practical Guide to Impractical Pets (with Emil Dolensek, D.V.M.)

An Insider's Guide to Cat Care

THE MORRIS APPROACH

BY BARBARA BURN   *Edited by Morris the Cat*

WILLIAM MORROW AND COMPANY, INC.   NEW YORK   1980

All photos by Bob Elmore

Library of Congress Cataloging in Publication Data
Burn, Barbara, 1940–
The Morris approach.
Bibliography: p.
1. Cats. I. Title.
SF447.B84 636.8 80-14051
ISBN 0-688-03693-7

Printed in the United States of America

First Edition

1 2 3 4 5 6 7 8 9 10

BOOK DESIGN BY SALLIE BALDWIN, ANTLER & BALDWIN, INC.

Contents

Editing this book was kind of fun. At least it was a good way to fill up the time between meals!

Editor's Foreword

There are a lot of advantages in being a superstar. Humans and cats the world around recognize me wherever I go and always give me preferred seating in restaurants or theaters; fans tend to serve me stuff like shrimp cocktail when I dine out; my staff keeps me groomed and gorgeous. It's first class all the way. But there are responsibilities, too. My mailbox is constantly full of letters asking for advice and information: What does "finicky" really mean, and how can I be it? How do you keep your nails trimmed without getting swacked for scratching the upholstery? Do you sleep in the nude and use a litter box like the rest of us?

The first few months of answering the letters were kind of fun since I love to give advice, especially to cats who haven't mastered the art of keeping their humans in line, but eventually I got tired of repeating myself. And when I recommended one of the many available books on cat care, I was told that the authors of those books had somehow missed the point. And it's true. For every piece of cat-care advice I've read in those books, there is a cat I know who is an exception. The reason should be clear—those books were written from the human point of view, as if humans were endowed with superior insight into what cats are like and what they need in order to be healthy and happy. Even I will admit that some humans know more than others, but show me one who can tell you what it really feels like to be a cat purring or who can explain why a litter of five kittens, raised the same way, should turn into five very different adult cats. I don't claim to understand the science of genetics, and I don't sprinkle my cocktail-party chatter with words like "rhinotracheitis" (mainly because I don't pronounce it very well); but I can assure you that any cat—from the streetwise tabby to the aristocratic purebred—knows a great deal more about being a cat than any human does. The problem is that cats almost never have a chance to read manuscripts before they go to the printer.

And so, folks, here is the inside story—a sensible book about cat care addressed to humans and felines alike, taken straight from the cat's mouth, so to speak. Thanks to the opportunities I've had to be myself in front of an entire nation, I have been able to teach people—the way I trained my own human—that it was okay for cats to be finicky. Fan letters assured me that owners no longer were annoyed when their cats didn't eat everything with grace and gratitude. It became fashionable—no, essential—that cats show individual character and act choosy about their food. Because their humans were listening to me, they began to listen to their own cats and to spend more time and effort to provide acceptable dinners. But food isn't the only thing in a cat's life (it may be the most important *thing, but it's not all there is). At last this book will give me a chance to expound on the total Morris Approach, my very own philosophy that will allow each and every cat to become completely himself.*

Unfortunately I do not type well (it tends to dull my claws), and no printer I know can read my paw-writing, so I have been obliged to obtain the services of a human assistant in order to get my Approach down on paper. Although she naturally came equipped with human attitudes as well as a typewriter, I have, I believe, kept her under enough control to make this book authentic. She spent weeks studying me and taking notes on everything I did and said, and, in spite of my natural modesty and reticence, she managed to capture most of the real me. I found it necessary to speak directly to the reader from time to time in the book (you can tell my own words from the different kind of typeface), and she was willing to allow me to edit her words where I saw fit, as I often did. We had a terrific argument about the matter of gender (she wanted the feminine pronoun throughout, but I insisted on the masculine, though I was generous enough to allow her to refer to a mother cat as a "she"), but for the most part we got along as well as one could expect. Because we found it necessary to generalize in this book, in spite of our belief that each cat is an individual, we encourage the reader to keep in mind that any single cat may not follow form exactly. We recommend that you listen to your own cat before you make up your mind about what is best for him. Better than that, we recommend that you let your cat read this book as well. We wouldn't be surprised, in fact, if your cat were trying at this very moment to get into your lap to take a look for himself.

—Morris the Cat

1

The Cat-Human Relationship

Or, how to adjust humans to the fact that people need cats more than we need them

Any self-respecting feline (and what cat is not self-respecting?) will tell you that humans are not particularly necessary (though they're often amusing). Of course, they're okay for dishing up "din-din" and for providing those creature comforts that require the use of a can opener or a shopping cart.

Cats are not naturally social—in the wild, they are generally solitary animals and do not live in herds or packs—so to humans, cats may appear to be standoffish and difficult to get to know. Their appeal is a special one. The secret is to take them on their own terms, not on ours. How could a human fail to be honored when a cat, who is quite capable of living independently, chooses to move in and live with him? Put another way, what could be more rewarding than to be loved by a cat?

There's a great deal that a cat can offer a human partner. In addition to being self-sufficient, cats are clean and reliable, beautiful to look at, fun to play with, and enormously comforting to hold. There is nothing quite so tranquilizing as a purring cat in one's lap, so absorbing as the sight of an elegant feline striking a graceful pose. And certainly there is no gesture so touching as a gentle nudge from a feline friend.

Although a cat will move into your house and will give you endless hours of enjoyment for little effort on your part, there are certain responsibilities involved in keeping a cat if the cat-human relationship is to be satisfying for both parties.

While a cat can be as lovely to look at as a porcelain statue, a beautiful cat nonetheless defies you to put him on a pedestal, for he has a few habits that may not please the utter aesthete. I remember someone telling me how beautiful she thought my Siamese cat would look in the Oriental decor of her living room. I remember equally well the expression of horror that came across her face when we paid a visit, for the cat not only moved about but actually jumped up to inspect the collection of Oriental antiques on her mantelpiece. (She was lucky we didn't stay long enough to do a job on her needlepoint pillows!) Moving about, shedding, and scratching things are perfectly natural activities for a cat, but a human who wants to coexist with bric-a-brac and upholstery *and* with a cat will have to learn to cope. Cats are aesthetes in their own way, too; at least they are fastidious when it comes to personal cleanliness. In a human household, however, they have to rely on the hygienic instincts of the one who can work the faucets to keep their food and water dishes and litter boxes clean.

Although some cats will do their best to keep emotions to a minimum, all cats have them and will need some attention on a daily basis. Outdoor cats can explore, hunt, and otherwise get their natural feline kicks, but indoor cats need something to do other than waddle over to the food dish every so often. If you are away from home all day, don't be surprised if your cat seems wide-awake at night just when you want to get some sleep. He probably took a catnap during the day. When you plan to be away, see that the cat has something or someone interesting to play with, and be sure that you are generous with your affection when you are around. Cats are not demanding of your attention the way dogs are—constantly looking for a companion to go for a walk, for example—but don't take advantage of feline self-confidence. Beneath that aloof exterior beats a warm heart, and it's up to you to tap that considerable resource. As we will illustrate in the chapters that follow, giving a cat a good life in the form of nutritious food, daily care, and affection is not a big deal for a human; in fact, once you get the household equipped and the daily routine established, you'll find that life should be a good deal for you both. Luckily, one of the major responsibilities—that of maintaining morale and keeping the household operating smoothly—is most definitely the cat's, as Morris is about to explain.

HOW TO REMIND HUMANS THAT THEY NEED YOU

Cats know how essential they are to humans, but insensitive two-legged types are all too likely to forget this fact unless reminded. Don't bother to leave little notes around the house ("Please feed me" is the kind of note that only a dog would write) or make plaintive little cries and put on forlorn facial expressions. Here are a few guidelines for the secure cat who wants to pass his self-confidence along to his human.

When you haven't been fed lately and your human is walking in the direction of the kitchen, weave in and around his legs until noticed. Do not trip him, but do not give up.

When your human is reading and paying no attention to you, lie down on the book or newspaper and stretch out. This is especially effective if the human is doing a crossword puzzle because you may get to play with the pencil.

If your human is sleeping comfortably and you aren't, lie on his chest and breathe. (This is particularly interesting after you've eaten tuna fish.) If nothing occurs, gently pat the face with your paw, claws retracted. If the human is lying on his stomach, curl around the pillow until he has trouble breathing. When he awakes, purr.

I've always made a point of being well read—it keeps my human on his toes.

2
Understanding Your Cat

Or, how to keep the upper paw at all times

(EDITOR'S NOTE: Cats who wish to retain control should read this before their humans do)

Cat people (and some cats we know) say that cats are unique, special, independent, elegant, discriminating, confident, proud, self-respecting, and finicky. People who don't understand cats will call them unfriendly, unfeeling, sneaky, cruel, and untrustworthy. These people were probably mice in earlier reincarnations. In fact, cats are perhaps more straightforward and honest than the average dog, but because cats are not naturally social animals, they have not developed the usual social amenities of dogs and humans. Cocktail-party chatter, small talk, superficial smiles, and little white lies are not necessary in cat circles. This lack of what some call the social graces (and what we call dis-graces) has made the cat extremely easy to read if you know how to interpret the gestures. Unlike a fearful dog that may wag its tail, lower its head in submission, and then bite without warning, a cat will always let you know what he's going to do. Only in an extreme situation will a cat actually bite or scratch seriously, but even then he will have given good and sufficient warning in the form of a hiss, a flicking tail, slitted eyes, and flattened ears. In some ways the threat is more frightening than the actual attack!

Because cats don't naturally live in social groups, it is not part of their personality to please others, to be grateful, or to act submissive, and so they do not seem to be very easily trainable. If you can understand that about your cat, you won't feel offended when dinnertime comes and goes and he hasn't even given you so much as a purr for your trouble.

It should be clear, though, that cats are easy to understand if you know the language. Cats may not speak like humans, but they certainly have a large vocabulary if you think of the various parts of their bodies as extensions of their vocal cords. Here is a guide for those humans with a curiosity about cat language.

A GLOSSARY OF CAT LANGUAGE

Any human possessing a decent dictionary can get along in a foreign country. In fact, most humans would not travel abroad without one. Yet right at home the human is often helpless when it comes to understanding the cat. This is not a question of foreign accents, poor grammar, or even awkward sentence construction; it's a basic matter of vocabulary, which the average human simply doesn't comprehend. A dog will do its best to learn English, but a cat feels that he doesn't have to do so. If the human doesn't understand, then that's the human's loss. But Morris has deigned to explain the most important nuances of cat language—they're interpreted here in terms any human can understand.

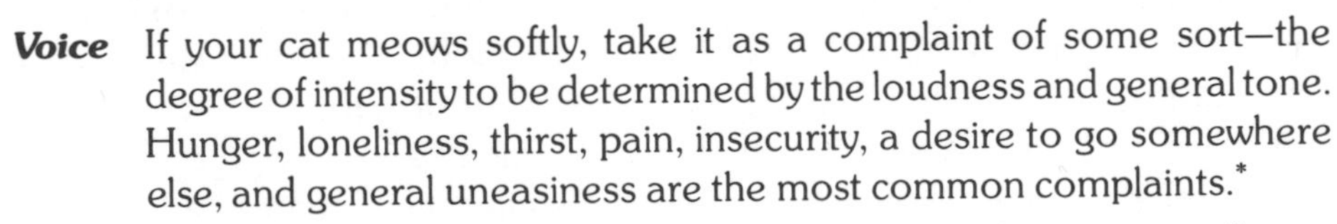

Voice If your cat meows softly, take it as a complaint of some sort—the degree of intensity to be determined by the loudness and general tone. Hunger, loneliness, thirst, pain, insecurity, a desire to go somewhere else, and general uneasiness are the most common complaints.*

If your cat purrs, this is a sign of contentment. Some cats will purr when spoken to affectionately; others will do so only when stroked gently or rubbed behind the ears.

If your cat screams, a most disconcerting sound, something important is going on—breeding, fighting, or agony. It is an alarm and should be responded to as such.

Eyes When your cat closes his eyes without going to sleep and his ears are upright, he is expressing trust and a sense of utter well-being. Enjoy the compliment.

* Siamese cats are exceptions in the vocal department. They "talk" almost constantly, but especially when spoken to. Female Siamese in heat have been compared, unfavorably but accurately, to wailing Banshees. As with a human friend who talks too much, take a Siamese conversation with a grain of salt or get earplugs.

When your cat narrows his eyes to a slit so that the pupils look like pinpoints and his ears are flattened, he is expressing utter fury and aggression. Steer clear.

A cat with suddenly wide-opened eyes and dilated pupils is watchful and possibly afraid, but he could be angry. Be on your best behavior.

Ears When ears are upright and straight ahead, your cat is probably contented and tuning out, though an intent expression means that he is concentrating on something or at least curious about it.

When his ears are flattened, your cat is angry. Flat back means aggression; flat forward means fighting; flat sideways means submission but not of the voluntary variety.

When his ears are moving all about, your cat is alert to his surroundings and may be on guard.

Body An arched back coupled with a fuzzed-up coat and tail and a sideways movement means that your cat is defensive, fearful, and likely to become aggressive. This is his way of trying to look as large as possible and to threaten the enemy into flight. If this doesn't work, your cat may either attack or flee; this is common in kittens, rarer in adult cats.

An arched back with a tail held high and no bristled fur means that your cat wants to be stroked and is feeling rather friendly.

If your cat is slinking down and creeping along practically on his belly, he is stalking something and will soon leap and attack.

A stiff-legged walk looks haughty and insulting. It is meant to look that way, because that's just how your cat is feeling.

Paws An extended paw with no sign of a claw means that your cat needs some attention, perhaps even affection. Use your own paw to respond in kind.

An extended paw with claws in full display should be taken as a sign of aggression. Keep your paws to yourself.

A kneading gesture with the paws when your cat is sitting comfortably in your lap is a throwback to kittenhood, when the paws were used to keep the milk flowing during nursing. Often a cat who is weaned too soon from its mother will continue this behavior as an adult.

Tail Held straight up, your cat's tail is signaling contentment and friendliness.

A tail held straight out horizontally is attached to a stalking hunter.

If his tail is curled around your sitting cat's feet, you are being treated to an elegant pose; your cat is alert and watching for something, perhaps just a compliment.

If his tail is being flicked about, your cat is watchful but probably doesn't trust what he's watching. If the tail movement becomes quite active, your cat is becoming aggressive and will probably hiss.

If his tail is bristly or fuzzed up, your cat is afraid.

If his tail is held between his hind legs, your cat is abject and feeling sorry for himself. This is extremely rare.

Cats and People

If you have mastered the art of listening to a cat, you'll probably have a pretty good relationship with every cat you meet, at least certainly your own cat. But how will your cat relate to other people? Not all cat owners live alone, and not all cats can have the luxury of a single human. If a cat is introduced to a family of humans in kittenhood, he should have no trouble adjusting himself to several people, even children who may not be expert in handling such small live creatures. An older cat may take longer to adjust; some dignified cats I know feel that children move much too fast and are too noisy, but they usually learned to cope once the kids learned to treat them properly. Parents should be careful to teach children how to carry a cat (in the arms, fully supported by the hands and *not* by the scruff of the neck or, heaven forbid, the tail) and to treat every cat with both respect and gentleness.

It is probably easier for cats to adjust to unfamiliar adult humans than to children, though it isn't always easy for some humans to adjust to cats. Morris has a few pointed words below about the treatment of an ailurophobe (one who fears cats), but if you are concerned about a cat-hating friend, the only thing you can do is to encourage the friend to learn something about cats before jumping to conclusions. Cats can be very sensitive to people who don't like them and will often show their displeasure in no uncertain terms.

I have heard stories about cats who developed real cases of jealousy when their humans brought home new friends or spouses, but these all were cured in time. Either the cat was given his full share of affection by his human and treated properly and respectfully by the newcomer, or the newcomer gave up and went away. Morris has some advice on dealing with dubious humans.

CAT MEETS AILUROPHOBE

If your human is having company and if that company comes in the form of someone who doesn't like cats, you may have a very interesting evening ahead.

> *Unlike your usual approach, don't wait under the couch until the guest is comfortable. Meet him in the hall, and rub against his legs. This will put him at a disadvantage immediately.*
>
> *Once the guest is seated, jump into his lap, and sit there purring. When your human acts surprised and says something like "Well, he never does that with strangers!" just smile and purr some more. Then get down and go out to the kitchen as if you were going to stir the sauce or help make the salad dressing.*
>
> *During dinner, jump on the table. Even if you have never jumped on the dinner table before, do it now. Listen to your human say, "But he never does that! Really!" Smile again, check out the food, and jump off. As if the sauce didn't turn out quite right.*
>
> *After dinner, while the guest is enjoying his brandy and cigar by the fire, go into the bedroom and lie on his coat. Stay there until he leaves, making sure that you've gotten a month's supply of cat hair all over it.*
>
> *As he puts on his coat, scram. Stay out of sight until he is out of sight. You'll probably never see him again. Good riddance.*

Cats and Cats

People who work all day or spend a lot of time away from home run the risk of cheating their cats of the attention they need. Sometimes bored, lonely cats develop habits that may not be particularly attractive. Rather than punish a cat in an attempt to train him, the human will have better luck if he or she simply doubles the usual dose of attention or gives the cat a companion—preferably another cat. Not only will another cat afford companionship, a grooming partner, and someone to play with, but the human will probably notice that the bad habits will stop, food finickiness will diminish, and the amount of cat hair will double.

If you should decide to get a second cat, do not assume that your *numero uno* will put out a welcome mat, however. Some cats do not like each other on sight and will spend a few days hissing and scrapping to establish a working relationship, let alone a playful one. Older cats are often more tolerant of kittens than of other full-grown cats; in fact, if you're lucky, a young newcomer may take years off an old cat (though some older cats *never* adjust). Neutered animals are usually less likely to overreact to other neutered cats. (Toms and unspayed females, of course, will get along just fine, but your cat population will multiply fast—something you may not be prepared for.) Don't try to interfere if your two tabbies seem to hate each other and hiss or make other threatening gestures. In most cases the end result will be perfectly satisfactory, although if peace does not reign within a couple of weeks, you may have two truly incompatible cats and should consider finding a new home for one of them. In any event, treat each cat with equal attention and reassurance, and don't try to stick up for the undercat or play favorites. Be sure that you have separate food and water dishes for each animal, and perhaps more important, see that each one has a sleeping place of his own.

Cat fights can be terrifying to watch—the fur really does fly—and there is little a human can do to prevent them except to keep the cats separated. Do not try to separate cats in the heat of battle, for you could get badly scratched; pour a pan of cold water or drape a heavy blanket over the fighters to stop them. Though free-roaming outdoor cats will often come home with battle scars, fighting between indoor cats is rare.

Cats and Dogs

Since canines are a specialty of Morris's, I've let him speak a few words of his own on the subject.

Some humans think they're doing their cat a favor by getting him a pet dog. Personally I prefer a bird or fish, but if you end up with a canine, here are a few tips.

If you get a puppy, offer to make him feel at home. Show him what part of the house is his (the basement) and what part is yours (everything else). Tell him your human just loves to go for walks in the rain and cold. (And when your human takes the dog for an early-morning walk, stand by your litter box to point up its convenience features.) Teach the dog to fetch your toys for you (as long as he's not one of those slobbering types).

If you get a full-grown dog (I've seen some that resemble the Incredible Hulk), you've got a bigger problem on your paws. But don't worry. If your human is the sensitive type—and most cat lovers are—he'll probably figure you are upset by your new "rival." (Actually, cats are not competitive; we're superior.) Take advantage of it. Look depressed, and hold out for some new toys—catnip, gourmet food, flowers, a diamond collar . . .

Other Animals

Birds are natural prey for cats and should be kept well out of reach—and, if possible, out of sight. Small rodents, such as white mice, hamsters, and gerbils, can also be potential victims of the cat who learns to deal with the intricacies of cage-door latches, and they, too, should be kept out of harm's way. Larger animals, such as rabbits and guinea pigs, may not be in danger, but don't let them play with the cat unsupervised. And in spite of what Morris says, dogs and cats can coexist perfectly well if properly introduced, preferably at an early age. Dogs can be trained not to chase cats, for one thing, though it is difficult to teach a cat not to tease a dog.

The Great Outdoors

Some people feel that they are cheating their cats of natural experiences if they keep them cooped up all day. But as attractive as the outdoors is, with its birds and mice, its neighborhood cats, its trees to climb, and its alleyways to

A dog is never truly happy without someone in the family whom he can respect.

explore, the perils that lie outside are endless. While a cat who has had the chance to develop a thick hair coat won't suffer much in the cold and will usually be able to find a nice warm place out of the rain and sleet, even the healthy cat can become exposed to disease, develop internal parasites (worms) and external ones (fleas and ticks), or become poisoned by anything from insecticide-covered grass to the contents of a neighbor's garbage can. Dogs, automobiles, tough tomcats, and abusive humans are natural predators for the outdoor cat.

Although by comparison the social life of an indoor cat tends to be fairly limited, kittens brought up inside never miss what they've never known, and they tend to live longer and in better health. Although Morris roamed in the open before he arrived at the shelter from which he was adopted, he much prefers the indoor life if only because he feels he deserves the luxury that home offers. Your cat deserves this luxury, too. Don't feel sorry for your cat if he seems to spend all day looking out the window. It's not that the grass is greener out there (he may not even know what grass *is!*); it's just that he's watching his own brand of television. The wise human need only make a decision about the indoor-outdoor question before the cat moves in—or out, as the case may be. And once you have chosen the area that your cat will live in, you can be sure that he will assert his feline rights, making it his own domain.

WELCOME

3
Selecting a Cat

Or, selecting an owner

Most people assume they are the ones who do the selecting when it comes to bringing a feline into the family. Most cats, however, know that while it is tactful to allow humans to believe this, selection is a one-sided affair—it is the cat's side that counts. Whether the human looks for a cat in a pet shop, a humane shelter, or at a friend's home, the process is clearly in the capable paws of the cat, even if that cat is only a tiny kitten. If you accept this, you have passed the cat's first test of a human with flying colors. If you chuckle and doubt, read on.

Ask anyone who lives with a cat what made him or her choose that particular animal. Chances are that the answers will fall along these lines: "This was the cat who came over to me and acted friendly," "This cat seemed to be the smartest (or cutest or most active) in the litter," or "This cat just seemed to need me the most."

Any cat worth his nine lives is capable of putting on all sorts of different faces at will. All cats and kittens in need of a home can be friendly, bright, cute, lively, and helpless—unless, of course, they are wild, ill, or suffering from past abuse. The point is that a cat may choose one particular moment to play the part of the desirable cat, on the basis of his perceptive sizing up of the prospective human. Never underestimate the power of the kitten looking for a suitable home.

People (and cats) differ on what makes the ideal cat, but in spite of the

reaking in a new owner is an important responsibility for a cat. I
ways find that a warm welcome makes a human feel right at home.

one-sided nature of the selection process, the human prospect should keep a few things in mind. Age is one consideration; sex and breed are others. If you are prepared for a pet that will need to be fed three or more times a day and will get into every conceivable nook of your home (even those you didn't know you had), you're an acceptable human for a kitten, who will repay you with endless hours of amusement. If you're more of a sedentary type, you'd better opt for an older cat. If you want to breed cats, you will want an unneutered male and female (and a much more complete book than this one, since cat breeding should be considered a profession, not a hobby, unless you know exactly what you are going to do with the kittens). If you just want a cat companion, you'll want a neutered cat, in which case gender will be purely a matter of personal taste.

Morris would have you believe that good breeding in cats is a matter of good taste (damask rather than plastic slipcovers, for example), table manners (never use a knife and fork), and self-respect (if you don't, no one else will). He feels that people who have purebred cats do so only out of a need to claim that at least one member of the family has a lengthy pedigree.

Cat people, however, are usually somewhat less opinionated than Morris. There are reasons to have purebred cats: an interest in showing or breeding, a need to have some idea about what a kitten's looks and temperament will be like when he matures, and an overwhelming desire to spend a lot of money for a cat. The average cat person, however, if there is any such thing, is perfectly happy with a purring companion regardless of its price tag.

The most important quality of the ideal cat—everyone's ideal—is good health. Tiny, weak-looking, weepy-eyed kittens will break your heart, but try to harden yourself, for with a sickly kitten, more heartbreak will follow, to say nothing of veterinary bills. Look for a cat with clear, bright eyes, an alert disposition, a smooth coat with no bald patches or signs of scaly or flaky skin—and be sure that you take the cat to a veterinarian as soon as possible for an examination and for the inoculations that will keep him healthy. (See "Medical Matters" in Chapter 7.) If a cat should stray into your life, have a vet check him out right away; if you have other cats, don't bring the stray into the house until he has been given a clean bill of health. Neither Morris—a former stray turned superstar—nor I would ever suggest that you pass by a cat in trouble, but we do recommend that you be realistic about the possibility of serious illness.

THE MORRIS APPROACH TO CHOOSING AN OWNER

Selecting a suitable human is a relatively simple matter—your superior feline instincts should lead you to a good home. Here are some surefire interviewing techniques to see you through those first awkward moments with a prospective owner:

If a human approaches you as if to shake hands, turn away. He wants a dog. You want someone who will allow you to make the first move and who will appreciate that the first move in no way resembles a handshake. Act alert and friendly, but not too friendly or he'll think you are a dog. If all goes well, rub your head and body along his leg, and hold your tail straight up in the air. It gets them every time.

If you want to reassure your human that you are healthy as well as wise, do the following: Get your coat into the peak of condition, and clean your teeth; a gum massage isn't a bad idea since some knowledgeable humans will also look for pink, healthy gums. Do not scratch yourself in his presence. Do not allow your eyes or your nose to run, and refrain from sneezing.

If the human starts cooing over you and using baby talk (as in "din-din"), act aloof, though interested. This person may want a stuffed toy animal rather than a living, breathing feline, but don't take any chances. "Din-din," after all, means food in any language. Whatever you do, however, do not lapse into kitten talk or coo back. If you're going to train the human properly into serving suitable meals, you will have to retain control and remain dignified.

If the human puts you through a series of tests, test him right back. When he drops an object behind you to see how alert you are or to ascertain that you are not deaf, look at the object scornfully as if the human had just dropped it out of clumsiness, thus testing his self-confidence. If he bats a piece of crinkly paper at you to see if you are playful, bat it right back to test his reflexes. If he misses, remind yourself to establish an exercise program when you get home.

4

Household Management

Or, how to manage your human and a household at the same time

The cat who has chosen his human well knows what to expect and how to adapt himself long before his perceptive paws touch the welcome mat. If the human is a loner with unusual habits and a nonconformist's attitude toward life, the cat will be more than happy to go along. If the human is a sociable sort with regular routines and good manners, the cat will make the appropriate adjustments. But do not be misled by the inconspicuous way in which a cat will work his way into your home and into your life-style. Do not assume that this cooperative behavior means you will ever be the same again. Remember what Morris says: "A cat who is too cooperative soon loses control of his owner." All cats know that the human's home is the cat's castle.

Has it ever occurred to you why some landlords specifically forbid tenants to keep cats? This is not because they are noisy or dirty, since no cat is either. It is because landlords are extremely sensitive to the fact of cat dominance. Though no money changes hands when a cat moves in, and no feline signatures become affixed to the lease, the property in which the cat lives somehow inevitably becomes the cat's. No sensible landlord wants to accept that, and no human partner in a cat relationship can afford to forget it.

It behooves the intelligent human, therefore, to make the household as suitable as possible for the new owner, providing a few standard items of furniture and equipment and making a few alterations in the daily routine. It is a good idea to install these before the cat installs himself, even if only to avoid

eading the lease is hard on the eyes, but it impresses the landlord. (It
lso pays to check out the "no dogs" claws, er, clause.)

arguments about the color of the food dishes and other major struggles, the loss of which could be terribly demoralizing. (Don't bother to ask to whom.)

Like yourself, a cat will require things to eat and drink from, places to sleep and eliminate, modes of travel, and means by which to keep beautiful, healthy, and physically fit. How elaborate these are will depend on the human's taste, self-image, and bank account.

Morris has graciously agreed to provide a consumer's guide to cat equipment on the condition that I give you some hints on how these items should be used (he already knows).

Dishes *Two at least, one for food and the other for water. Made of sturdy material, untippable, unrustable, and unbreakable. Royal Doulton is nice, but humans are liable to break it; plastic is déclassé but okay so long as it's kept clean and is filled when you're ready to eat; stainless steel or aluminum is probably the best because you can make a terrible racket with either when the dishes are empty.*

Keep the water dish full at all times with clean water, and empty the food dish after mealtime unless you use only dry food or have a desire to feed other small animals, too. Keep both dishes in the same place so that the cat needn't hunt for its food the way it hunts for mice. Finickiness is a natural cat characteristic, and there's no need to encourage it.

Bed *This can be placed anywhere and made of anything so long as it is quiet, warm, and impeccably clean. I prefer to sleep as high up in a room as possible (it's the leopard in my blood), unless I feel like taking the lion's share of the biggest bed in the house.*

Softness of material doesn't matter to many cats; some will make themselves comfortable on a radiator so long as it's warm and draft-free and out of the way of traffic. Nor does the exact location matter, though many cats prefer their human's bed to their own unless convinced otherwise, usually by a hyperactive sleeper. If the cat seems to ignore his own bed in spite of your urging, let him choose a favorite spot and move his blanket or other bedding there; if the cat still prefers your bed, you can always move yourself to the radiator. If your cat uses special bedding material, be sure that it is not only washable but washed, at least once a month.

Toilet *If indoors, I like my litter box right in the living room where I can get at it. Ash-filled fireplaces and potted plants are also good. If outdoors, I like the kids' sandbox. The container doesn't matter (it can be a plastic dishpan or a porcelain tub) so long as it's filled with two inches of nice, scratchy material that can be easily kicked over the side which will remind my human to clean it out daily. Without fail. The litter material can be that clay-based stuff (gritty and gray), alfalfa (green and pleasant-smelling—for a while), or shredded newspaper. Some people say that the lead-based newsprint is bad for tender felines, but I say that the funnies and the editorial page are definitely good bathroom material.*

Cats are meticulous when it comes to toilet habits; that's why they like the litter material which they use as a natural cover-up. That's also why cats are so easy to train; if their mothers don't teach them, one quick lesson from you after mealtime is all it takes. (See the next chapter for instructions.) As for fireplaces and plants, take precautions if you wish. Some litter pans come with special tops to prevent litter overflow, although newspaper spread under a plain pan will help keep the stuff from being tracked through the house. I do not personally recommend keeping the litter box in the middle of the living room. Any out-of-the-way but accessible place will do.

Cat Carrier *If a Rolls-Royce is not available, anything that is sturdy, ventilated, and monogrammed will serve my purposes adequately. Lightweight material will be appreciated by the human cat-carrier carrier, but I refuse to be seen in a cardboard case which is easily torn apart and becomes soggy in damp weather. Where size is concerned, less is more; a huge case makes me feel a bit nervous in motion, while one that is just big enough for me to stand up, turn around and stretch out in is fine.*

A cat carrier is an important piece of equipment. Large purses, shopping bags, and boxes may do in a pinch, but they are designed for something other than cat carrying and are not recommended. Commercially made carriers are available in most pet shops and come in a variety of shapes and sizes at reasonable prices. Plastic or fiber glass cases are probably the best—lightweight, sturdily constructured, and properly designed with ventilation holes, strong handles, and windows for visibility. A soft, absorbent lining of cloth or shredded paper is comforting and comfortable and can be removed for cleaning or replacement; a familiar cat toy or two may be comforting as well. Be sure that the case is furnished with an identification label or tag with your name and address clearly marked on it. Don't neglect getting one of these cases even if you aren't the traveling type; a cat will need to take occasional trips to the vet, and carrying him in your arms is just asking for trouble. Even the calmest cat will become disoriented away from home and can scratch his way free into what may become oblivion. (See Chapter 8 for traveling tips.)

Collars

When indoors, I prefer to present myself unadorned (who could improve on nature anyway?), but outside I always wear an identification collar, even though I'm usually recognized instantly on the street wherever I go.

Because outdoor cats tend to wander through narrow passageways and climb trees, the collar should be made with an elasticized section so that it can expand and allow the cat to escape if it should get hung up on something. These collars are not designed to expand with growth, however, so if you have a kitten, be sure to check for fit occasionally, and purchase a new collar when you can no longer fit two fingers comfortably between collar and cat. Flea collars should be worn only on the advice of a veterinarian; some may actually be toxic to your cat, and in any case a collar would be a needless expense if your cat hasn't been exposed to fleas.

Grooming Tools

My favorite and most effective beauty aid is my own tongue (eat your heart out, Estée Lauder), but I always enjoy a grooming session with my human. It's very comforting (reminds me of my dear old mum), and it also gives my human the chance to check me over for imperfections. A simple bristle brush is all I require—with a silver handle, of course. And nail clippers for the manicure.

Some of Morris's long-haired friends will be thankful for frequent brushings and combings with a steel comb as well as a brush. Otherwise, they get matted, and that may require the assistance of a pair of blunt scissors or, in extreme cases, a veterinarian. Most of Morris's human friends appreciate cat grooming, too, for it keeps shed cat hair to a minimum on furniture and clothing.

Scratching Post *I have had a fine old live oak installed in my living room for exercising my forearms and keeping my nails trim and honed to a fine edge. Less fortunate cats may make do with a commercially made scratching post or something homemade, but many of my down-and-out pals have ended up down and out of the house for trying out their claws on damask upholstery. The worst case, I know, however, is an old crony whose bad habits led his human to reupholster everything in Naugahyde.* Yecch.

Unless you get a kitten accustomed to the use of a scratching post early on, you may end up having to get Naugahyde upholstery yourself. The next chapter includes training advice.

Toys *Fans send me toys from all over—catnip toys, jigsaw puzzles, and games of Monopoly and Risk. My favorite toys, however, are crinkled bits of cellophane from cigarette packs, low-hanging spider plants, toes hidden under blankets, electric typewriters, and the stereo turntable. Catnip turns me on, too, though I prefer Dom Pérignon.*

Cats are born hunters and even as full-grown animals enjoy using their hunting instincts in play. Toys that roll, move, or swing are invariably fascinating, but take care that the objects themselves are not small or flimsy enough to be torn apart and swallowed. Some plants are toxic (see table on page 34), and anything electrical is a potential source of danger.

Plants *Sometimes after a good meal, I like to chew on some grass (not smoke, chew) or an attractive house plant and then to throw up on the carpet. This is perfectly natural; besides, it keeps everyone on his or her toes. I have finally trained my human to give me a plant of my own. I know it's mine because it has my name on it.*

Many cats share this habit with Morris; whether the grassy material serves as a digestive aid or a nutritional one is not entirely understood, but cat lovers with green thumbs know well that cats can

Kittens may walk on the keys, but, like any truly sophisticated cat, I always check to see whether the thing's in tune first.

often do great damage to plants for which they have developed a taste. The thoughtful cat person will provide a special pot of plain timothy grass for the cat or will add some vegetables to the diet.

Catproofing the Castle

All cats are curious, but curiosity needn't kill if you are well prepared. For example, you must remember that cats are expert climbers and jumpers and that open doors and drawers are perceived as open invitations to explore. A cat will figure that if it's open, it's to be walked, jumped, or sneaked through, and disaster may well lie on the other side. I have known kittens to work their way into sofa beds, ovens, clothes dryers, and dishwashers; I have known cats who have fallen from fire escapes, bookshelves, and mantelpieces and out of closets. Some cats will try to take everything with them as they go—dishes from the table, bric-a-brac from the sideboard, hanging plants from the ceiling, and whole chickens from the stovetop. Forgive me, Morris, but cats are not always the most graceful animals in the world, and though they may land on their feet, the crockery usually doesn't.

Electrical objects, such as hanging cords and light sockets, also hold an endless fascination for felines, especially kittens, and they can prove as bad for the cat as for the fixtures. See that sockets are well concealed behind pieces of furniture that can't be walked behind, and try to place lamps where they can't be tipped over. If you're in the habit of using sharp objects, you may have to become a compulsive picker-upper.

Although cats will do almost anything to avoid getting their fur wet, water standing in a tub, sink, or toilet may be a source of great interest to an inexperienced kitten, and the cautious human will prevent a drowning accident by keeping toilets covered and sinks empty when not in use.

Poisonous materials—such as certain plants, lead-based paint, cleaning fluids, and insecticides—are usually unattractive to cats if they smell bad, but some noxious plants, woods, and fabrics may seem irresistible and should be kept out of reach. Cats do not usually chew on things the way puppies do, but wool and tissue paper are often especially intriguing. Wool may retain enough animal odor to remind cats of their hunting past (though I personally have never seen a cat chase a full-sized sheep), and tissue paper, like onionskin paper and cellophane, may be deliciously crinkly in cat teeth; but these explanations pale in the face of destroyed woolen garments and confettilike bits of paper all over the rug. The alert human will store these items out of sight and out of feline mind.

Garbage is another potential source of danger. Even if the leftovers are perfectly harmless, the sight of an overturned garbage can is not a pleasant one for a human to behold (or clean up). Food left out on counters is, of course, considered a particular delicacy and falls within the rules of fair play, especially if it's something like butter that can simply be licked without anyone's noticing. But garbage cans should be carefully sealed against feline intervention, for they often hold more than food—pieces of broken glass, bits of plastic wrap, string, and aluminum foil, and other tidbits that could harm a curious cat.

POISONOUS PLANTS

Outdoors

arrow grass
bladder pod
brachen fern
buttercup
castor bean
chokecherry
cocklebur
corn cockle
crotalaria
iris
jimsonweed
laurel
lily of the valley
locoweed
nettle
nightshade
oleander
poison vetch
rattlebush
rhododendron
sensitive fern
water hemlock

Indoors

dieffenbachia (dumb cane)
philodendron
poinsettia
Plus anything with insecticide on it

Cat Caveat

The above is a basic list of commonly occurring plants that are poisonous to cats, but it should not be considered comprehensive.

EDIBLE GREENS

cat grass
marigolds
petunias
nasturtiums
timothy grass

Setting Up Schedules

There are few changes that you'll have to make in your regular schedule once the cat joins your household. Sure, you'll have to shop for cat food, but who doesn't make a trip to the supermarket once in a while anyway? Yes, you'll have to think about emptying the litter box and washing up the cat's supper dishes, but don't you make your bed and wash your own dishes? You comb your own hair, so what's the big deal about combing your cat's? Exercise for a cat is simply another word for fun and games—no jogging around the local running track or even walking outdoors in the middle of a rainy night as you'd have to do with a dog. Affection must be applied in liberal, regular doses, but the time for that is established by the cat, not the human.

Nevertheless, there are a few habits that should be adopted. Food must be served on a daily or twice daily basis (perhaps three times a day if you are feeding a kitten). The cat's personal equipment must be kept in a reasonable state of tidiness at all times—every cat does his best to keep himself clean, but it's not always possible for the cat to clean his belongings as well. Food and water dishes should be washed between meals, as mentioned earlier. The cat's bed, like your own, should be cleaned from time to time, perhaps weekly, and washed or cleaned thoroughly once a month. Even more important is the state of the litter box, which needs more frequent attention, or the cat may refuse to use it altogether, and your guests may begin to refuse your invitations. We recommend that you replace the litter material every other day, more often if you have more than one cat. Beneath the dry surface will be an accumulation of urine-soaked litter material, which can cause strong odor if not cleaned often. When you empty the box, don't just refill it with clean litter, but wash it out thoroughly with detergent and water, rinse, and dry. Don't bother to use a disinectant (some brands are not good for cats), but see that the box is odor-free before you put in more litter.*

The job of cleaning up after your cat is not difficult or time-consuming, and if you are a reasonably normal person, these routines should pose no problem. If you're abnormal, of course, your cat will soon have you in line.

* Pregnant women should avoid handling cat feces; the feces sometimes harbor the organism that causes the disease toxoplasmosis, which can be dangerous.

MORRIS'S GUIDE TO HUMAN HOUSEKEEPING

In spite of the fact that commercials for cleaning materials are more common (alas) than cat food commercials, humans have a lot to learn when it comes to keeping house for cats. Here are some tips for the conscientious feline who wishes to keep his human as fastidious as he is himself.

To make sure that the litter box gets changed regularly, master the art of picking up bits of litter in your paws and dropping them at crucial points between the bed and the bathroom (or wherever your human is in the habit of walking barefoot). If worse comes to worst, don't use the box at all, but try the bathtub. They'll get the idea.

If you feel that your water dish isn't being cleaned and refilled promptly enough, pretend that it's a stagnant pool. Never allow yourself to be seen drinking, but when your human goes to the sink and runs the water, jump into the sink, and try to drink from the faucet as if you had been in the desert for weeks.

If you aren't being groomed as much as you'd like, curl up on some colored fabric. This can be part of a piece of furniture, of course, but even better is a lap belonging to a human who is about to go out for a night on the town.

5
Moving Right In

And taking over

Now that you've been chosen by your cat and have prepared your household for the great arrival, the time has come to let the cat out of the bag (or preferably the carrier) and to give him a chance to decide whether his choice was a good one.

One of the first things for you to do is to decide what to call your cat (he will also decide what to call you). There are trends in cat names, just as there are in human circles, and we've even been seeing more feline Morrises over the past several years. The cat responsible for this fad has some additional thoughts for those who prefer not to be copycats.

My name is one of the most distinguished in the business. Naming your cat after me, though, would be asking him to live up to a legend. If your cat is a female, the name Morris will simply confuse her. I was named Morris because of the distinctive M *on my forehead—which also stands for masterful. Other cats also come with names written all over them—like Blackie, Mittens, and so on. Most have names known only to themselves, and it takes a very sensitive person to figure them out. A few unfortunate cats go through life bearing boring monikers like Tom and Tabby. Their humans haven't got any imagination.*

Exotic breeds often have exotic names—like Meow-Tse-Tongue. Many cats get unbearably cute ones—Twinkletoes or Fuzzy-Wuzzy (a cat I once knew by

the latter got a terrible case of dermatitis and lost most of his fur temporarily and, I believe, deliberately).

Cats owned by people with special hobbies or occupations often get unusual names (Gin and Bitters were a pair of kittens owned by one of my bartender buddies), while literary humans often pick their cats' names out of favorite books (Scarlett O'Haira was an elegant orange sex kitten who had a crush on me once). Latin lovers will appreciate a feline companion named Furcifer (even though it means scoundrel and may no longer be suitable once the cat has survived kittenhood). Whatever name you select, it should be appropriate to the cat, easy to say, and something both you and the cat will be willing to live with for years. As soon as you arrive at the right name, use it frequently and on all appropriate occasions—such as when you call him to dinner, which should be very often—and he will probably come running.

Getting to Know You

Let your cat wander around your place until his curiosity has been satisfied. You might make some effort to see that he is properly introduced to the food and water dishes, the litter box, and his very own bed—in that order—but otherwise, you should simply let your cat relax and feel at home. Nervous cats or kittens may take a few days to settle down, but if *you* are relaxed, they will eventually follow your cue. Try to keep to your regular schedules so that your cat can adapt to them quickly. For example, if you work all day, your cat might as well get used to being alone right off the bat rather than feel betrayed by your absence two or three days into the relationship. You might decide to feed your cat his main meal in the morning so that he will be likely to sleep all day while you're gone. Don't, however, leave your cat entirely alone for both day and evening at first; otherwise, he may assume that he would have been better off somewhere else.

The First Meal

Because the first day is crucial from the point of view of your cat's subsequent habits around the house, don't just feed him at any old time. Try to feed your cat his first meal at what will become the regular hour, and stick to it. Most cats appreciate two meals—one in the morning and one in the evening. Cats tend to be nibblers rather than gobblers, like dogs, so it's a good idea to

…e of the first things to do in a new household is to find a nice, private …ot where you won't be disturbed. I prefer the classics shelf myself, …ht there between Cato and Catullus.

keep dry food available during the day when hunger may strike without warning. But do make the presentation of wet food a daily ritual at a specific time. Water should, of course, always be available.

Every Litter Bit Helps

After your cat's first meal, keep an eye out to be sure that he uses the litter box properly. If he is an adult cat and knows where the box is, you shouldn't have any trouble. If you have a kitten that hasn't had the appropriate lessons from his mother, you may have to help out. After the meal, pick up the kitten, and place him in the litter box. Help him to paw at the litter material until he eliminates. Once the kitten has done so, the odor (even if it's so slight that you can't detect it) will keep him coming back regularly. If the kitten makes a mistake, don't punish him. Say "no" firmly, pick up the mistake and the kitten, and put them in the box. If you discover the mistake long after it was made, simply clean the spot with disinfectant (to remove odor), and watch the kitten to make sure that the mistake is not repeated.

Some cats will deliberately spray urine outside the box, a natural, if unappealing, habit common to adult cats that haven't been neutered, both male and female. This is a way in which the cat marks his or her territory, indicating that he or she has been in the vicinity. The odor can be horrible, and in an adult cat the habit is usually unbreakable except by neutering (see Chapter 9), though even this doesn't always do the trick. The solution to this problem, as well as some others, is to neuter a cat during his or her first year. Kittens that are neutered before sexual instincts develop (at around six or seven months) usually never get into the habit of spraying.

Cats may occasionally eliminate outside the litter box if it hasn't been emptied on schedule (they hate the smell as much as humans do) or if they're unusually troubled about something and trying to get your attention. But again, punishing a cat for making such a gesture is not an effective preventive. The best cure, of course, is to keep the litter box clean, but also it can be helpful to give your cat some special attention on a regular basis; it certainly can smooth ruffled fur. Cats who have access to the outdoors can be easily trained to eliminate outside if you let them out after each meal. Just be sure that you're on hand to let your cat out when he needs to go, or install a swinging door that he can operate himself when the spirit moves him.

Other First-Day Activities

The first day—or even the first week—will be too full of new experiences to begin any training session in earnest, but the sooner the cat learns the word "no," the better. Dog people have been saying for years that the fact that cats can't be trained proves they are a less intelligent species. This is misleading. Cats have their own special kind of intelligence, appropriate to the needs of the feline species—they aren't as easily trained as dogs because they simply aren't social by nature and don't have to play at pleasing anyone except themselves.

Nevertheless, it is perfectly possible to train a cat to do certain things if one is consistent and patient and, when appropriate, if one uses a reward system. If the dining-room table or the living-room sofa is to be considered out of bounds, you can make this clear to your cat by saying no firmly or by clapping your hands once or twice and removing him from the premises. Not just the first time, but *every* time he tries to get on the table or sofa. You'll never know what your cat does when you are out of the room, of course, except by the evidence of cat hair or paw prints, but chances are that if you find him on a forbidden spot and he has been told it's forbidden, he will jump off the moment you enter the room. Your cat may be trained, but he's just disobeying and expects to be told so.

Discipline is one form of training; learning tricks is quite another and can be instilled only by the reward principle. If your cat does something cute or clever, give him a bit of food or a pleasant stroking and a kind word, and it's likely that he will repeat the behavior. Maybe not right then but at some future time. Cats have been taught to do any number of marvelous things—flush the toilet, alert deaf people to ringing telephones or doorbells, and get their humans to open the refrigerator door. Some extraordinary cats have even learned how to act in television commercials—better than some professional human actors, if you want to know the truth.

TAKEOVER TRICKS

Once you have trained your human so that he feels he has established some basic routines and set up some rules, it's time to assert your mastery more overtly. Here are a couple of ways to let him know that the initial training

Possession is nine points of the law. As soon as my human gets adjusted to his little pillow on the floor, I think I'll ask him to get me some more appropriate sheets—satin was really what I had in mind.

program is going pretty well—and make him properly appreciative of your obvious superiority in these matters.

If your human is the type who has decided that one meal a day is all you need, change his mind. If you are supposed to forgo breakfast, try to participate in the enjoyment of his *morning meal—help scramble his eggs, catch the toast as it pops out of the toaster, etc. If you are fed in the morning but not at night, help set the table for his dinner. Move the forks and knives around, or, if worse comes to worst, rearrange the centerpiece—your taste in table settings is probably more imaginative than his anyway.*

Just before bedtime (you can tell the right moment when your human sets the alarm clock and turns out the lights), run (do not stalk) to the bed (his, not yours), and lie down in the middle of it. Stretch and luxuriate, purring loudly; then curl up and look more comfortable and contented than you ever have before. When your human tries to explain that your bed is the one over there on the floor, pretend not to understand and purr louder. Do not move—if you're lucky, he may be too sleepy to put up a fight.

6
Feline Foodstuffs

Or, how to eat your tuna and have it, too

Inexperienced cat people assume that cat food comes in two different kinds of packages: tin cans and mice. Experienced cat people know that the packages, as well as the contents, are endless in variety and that the nutritional value differs considerably from one type to the next. Thanks to the research sponsored by commercial pet-food companies, we know a great deal about the nutritional requirements of the normal cat. The cat food available in your supermarket is probably better for your cat than a homemade diet, which can be both expensive to prepare and deficient in some important ways, since cats need different nutrients from humans.* In selecting the best possible food for your cat, study the chart below and then read the labels on the packages in the market before you buy.

DAILY NUTRITIONAL REQUIREMENTS FOR CATS

1 combination of meat or fish, vegetables, minerals, and vitamins containing:

Water	70%	Carbohydrates	5%
Protein	14%	Calcium	0.6%
Fat	10%	Miscellaneous Minerals	

* Also, don't assume that a domestic cat can keep himself healthy on the mice in your barn or basement. Wild mice often carry diseases or harmful parasites. Besides, they don't usually show up on a regular, daily basis.

A straight diet of meat is as bad for a cat as a diet that has too little meat. Many people assume that serving up fresh beef kidneys, chicken livers, or crabmeat is somehow a life enhancer, but actually they are probably killing their cats with kindness. The best diet for a cat combines meat protein with other types of food, and this is what most commercial cat foods contain. Because cats, unlike dogs, thrive on variety, you should try to vary the diet with different flavors of food in order to provide complete nutrition.

But if you know Morris, you know this already. "Finicky" in cat language means being selective and having good taste, and Morris is no fool. He knows that a diet of pure tuna fish would be bad for him, but because he tends to have trouble explaining this to his human, he has to act it out. Don't force your cat to do the same thing. (Morris wouldn't care for the competition anyway!)

Knowing what the nutritional requirements are is only half the battle, however. How do you select from the myriad cat foods that line your supermarket shelves? First of all, select a brand that you can trust. Some of the most reputable companies come by their fame for good reason; their foods are carefully tested for taste and nutritional value. Secondly, learn about the basic five different categories of nourishment that are available: dry, wet, semimoist, supplements, and liquids. Let's allow cat food expert Morris to describe them.

Dry Food *Good stuff. Sometimes a bit dry for my taste (only about 12 percent moisture), so I always accompany it with a bowl of good vintage water. But it is rich in nutrients (30 percent protein, 8 to 10 percent fat, plus minerals) and a good deal of food value for the money. It is also terrific for my teeth, keeping tartar accumulation to a minimum, so that they stay at their whitest, and my breath is at its freshest. Still, I don't care for a steady diet of dry food—too much of that particular good thing can disrupt feline digestion.**

What I like best about dry food, though, is that you can hear the box rattle from any part of the house, unlike a can, and that it is nice and easy for me to open if my human is a bit late getting dinner served and remembers to leave the box on the counter. Besides, humans don't mind leaving dry food out all day because it doesn't attract anyone but me, so I can eat whenever I want to. Which is often,

* Also, an *excess* of dry food in the feline diet can aggravate kidney and urinary-tract ailments.

Being finicky is not easy when there are so many good choices, but I think I'll hold out for Liver-and-Bacon tonight.

since I'm a natural nibbler, not a greedy gobbler like a dog. But I know the importance of feline good looks, and I'm smart enough to watch my own waistline and not overeat.

Wet Food *Although I still haven't learned how to operate a can opener, this stuff is my favorite. It has a lot of moisture in it (about 78 percent good old H_2O), and it smells wonderful. Not as highly concentrated as the dry food, but very tasty indeed. In fact, it has a higher grade of protein and is very digestible, so I recommend it especially to all my very young kitten friends and to senior citizens as well as to those in the prime of life. Not all brands contain the same quality of food, though, so I suggest that every cat teach his owner to read the labels before establishing a preference for one particular kind. (I recommend my private brand, 9-Lives.) Needless to say, you must demand a variety of flavors and act extremely finicky if you don't get it. I always insist on sufficient minerals, vitamins, and carbohydrates in my food, and so should you.*

In my early life as a carefree wanderer, leftover human food used to fascinate me, especially bits of crab cake and chicken leg. But now I figure that if my human won't eat it, why should I?

Semi-moist Food *A convenient snack and particularly good for trips because it keeps well. Most semimoist foods are complete and balanced diets—they're a good compromise for the cat who can't make up his mind. Nice flavors, too.*

Supplements *I've never been a pill popper myself and count on getting all the goodies I need at mealtime. I occasionally like a bit of cooked vegetable with dinner (when I don't get any, I chew on my human's prize spider plant), but other than that, I get extras only when my doctor recommends them. There are, I hear, special prescription diets for cats less fortunate than me healthwise, and some of my friends keep themselves sleek and fit by taking vitamins and fat supplements. But I've never found it necessary to improve on the well-rounded meals I demand as a regular routine.*

Liquids *Catnip gives a much better high than wine or whiskey, so my preferred drink is water. I've spent many an interesting hour in front of* *a leaky faucet, but the risk of getting my fur wet is simply too great to allow a close relationship with the stuff unless it's properly served in my own dish. Like all living creatures, I need a certain amount of moisture in my system to keep it in working order (generally 5 percent of my weight, 10 percent when I was a kitten), but feline evolution has seen to it that my body is designed to conserve water well. To keep my human from getting the idea that I really like water a lot, I usually wait until he is out of the room before I sip. (It should go without saying that I never lap water the way dogs do; that kind of enthusiasm just isn't my style, and besides, it's too messy and can splash the whiskers.) I prefer bottled spring water, but tap water will do if it's fresh and clean. I refuse all water that has been standing in a bowl for more than six hours.*

When I was a youngster, I really loved milk, but I can't take it now (something about the lactose in it gives me indigestion). Although I stand alone in most respects, I am like many adult cats in my feelings about milk, and I can't imagine why humans call it nature's perfect food. Cream isn't any better; I usually insist that my human spare no expense to keep me in luxury, but a bowl of cream—unlike a collar of diamonds—is just too rich for my blood.

Digestive Problems

Occasional vomiting is a fairly common cat activity—it's a way for the cat to get rid of the hair balls that can accumulate in his stomach. When a cat licks his fur during grooming, some of the hair is bound to be swallowed up and thus form hair balls. Eating plants often seems to help the cat with hair balls; that is why it's a good idea to provide a cat with some grass or bits of vegetable to chew on. Or you can put petroleum jelly on the cat's paws. When he licks it off, it will work as a lubricant in his stomach. Frequent vomiting, though, may indicate a serious case of lodged hair balls or a disease and warrants a call to the vet. For a cat stricken with diarrhea, withhold food for twenty-four hours, give him one-half teaspoon of Kaopectate three times a day, and keep water available. If the diarrhea persists for more than a day or blood is present, consult the vet (see Chapter 7).

Obesity

Feeding a cat too much food can sometimes be as dangerous as feeding the wrong kind because obesity can cause or aggravate serious medical problems. If you cannot easily feel your cat's ribs through the layer of fur, you may have a fat cat on your hands. Ask your vet's opinion on the matter at your next regular visit, and if he agrees that your cat is overweight, a diet is in order. Don't starve your cat, but reduce the daily fare by 5 or 10 percent until you feel that he has achieved a normal weight.

Some people hesitate to neuter their cats because they believe that obesity will result, but neutering doesn't cause this condition—overfeeding does. A lack of sexual appetite that naturally follows neutering often results in less daily exercise for your cat, and his food intake should correspondingly be reduced as well.

Serving Food

Knowing your cat's needs and becoming familiar with the different types of available food are still not the whole story of feline feeding. The way in which food is served as well as the amount given daily is important. Cold food is not appealing to cats because the odor and flavor are less prominent. There is no need to heat cat food since room temperature will do, but don't serve food directly from the refrigerator, or you may provoke a bad case of finickiness. And do be regular about mealtime.

Food and water dishes should, of course, be cleaned between meals; in any case most cats find their own leftovers exceedingly unappetizing. If your cat regularly leaves food in his dish, serve less the next time, and consider increasing the number of meals.

A cat who refuses to eat food may be ill or may simply be trying that old trick of cowing (we prefer to call this catting) his human into submission. If your cat won't eat, and if there are other symptoms that might indicate illness, such as vomiting, refusal to drink water, listlessness, etc., don't hesitate to call the vet. But if you have a strong feeling that your cat is perfectly healthy but just being fussy, don't give in. Be sure that the food you serve is of good quality and offers variety and that you are serving it at regular intervals. But don't be forced into tempting the cat with special treats, or you'll find that the meals will

Richelie
BUTTON
MUSHROOMS
PURPLE
9-Lives
CAT FOOD
Liver & Chicken
Dinner
IN HEAVY SYRU
9-Live
Savory Ste
9-Lives
CAT FOOD
TUNA
IN SAUCE
IBERIA
flan
SPANISH
DESSERT

start consisting of special treats, which would not make for good nutrition in the long run.

Morris, of course, has his own ideas on the subject.

MORRIS'S GUIDE TO FINE DINING

Being finicky can mean the difference between life and Life. Here are some tidbits of advice that may be just as nourishing to you as your next can of tuna.

When your human is eating dinner and your own meal hasn't been up to its usual high standard, jump up on the table, and take pains to pose near his plate with your tail carefully curled around your feet. Do not walk over to the dish or make any move in its direction, but stare directly and constantly at its contents. If this has no effect, watch your human's fork go back and forth from plate to mouth.

When your human comes home from the market, don't waste time giving your usual warm greeting. Check out the shopping bags immediately. If you are pleased with the purchases, watch your human put them away on the cat food shelf, and reward him by sneaking into the empty paper bag. This will amuse him for quite a few minutes, but don't overdo. If you are not pleased with the purchases, flick your tail and leave the room.

No matter where you are or what you are doing, when you hear a can opener touch metal or a box of dry food being taken from a shelf, trot promptly to the kitchen and wait expectantly by your dish. Even if it turns out that the can contains corn and the box contains cereal, do not whine or look disappointed. Continue to look expectant. Keep this up for an hour or more, if necessary.

NLY THREE CANS??!!
is human needs a shopper's helper.

Physical fitness is an important part of my routine—they tell me Arnold Schwarzenegger started out this way. . . .

7
Beauty and Physical Fitness

Or, how to live all nine lives to the fullest

Americans have become fanatics on the subject of human physical fitness, and it is appropriate that we should concern ourselves with the well-being of our cats, too. Good feline health also begins with good exercise, and even if you don't plan to jog with your cat or to do setting-up exercises together at the scratching post, you should at least be able to offer your cat the basics of feline fitness.

Cats don't really need a standard exercise regimen to keep themselves in peak condition. But they are instinctively active in their own way, and they generally have a refined sense of playfulness, which can be easily aroused by a human with the proper training.

Morris believes that some of the more common games that humans like to indulge in with their cats, such as fetch and chase-the-string, are mere kitten's play. In his opinion, serious adult games require initiative efforts on the part of the cat rather than the human. Here are some of his suggestions for ways of getting (and giving) good exercise.

Mantel Marching *If you feel that life is getting a bit dull, take a walk on the mantelpiece (or on a table) where there are knickknacks strewn artfully about. As soon as you get your human's attention, start to pick your way through the array. By this time he should be sitting up straight and holding his breath. Carry on for a minute or two, and then jump down. This exercise is great for building up your human's lung capacity.*

Football *If your human is trying to get his exercise watching football on television, jump on top of the set, and let your tail hang down in front of the screen. Swish it back and forth, and really give him something to watch. If you keep it up, he may actually get up and go for a walk. Do this only during the game itself; ignore instant replays and commercials (unless, of course, they are cat food commercials, in which case you should nonchalantly point your paw at the screen).*

The Gravity Game *If your life is empty of playthings, use your imagination. Pushing small objects off bedside tables is really fun—especially if they contain things like jewelry or contact lenses. This game is most effective if the falling objects clatter noisily to the floor—your human is sure to come running to inspect the damage. You should be prepared to run too, before he discovers it.*

Good Grooming

Cats love to groom themselves and also to be groomed by humans who know how to give the right strokes. Outdoor cats shed about twice a year, but indoor cats shed all year round and need human assistance to avoid hairy situations. Grooming prevents mats and tangles from developing in long-haired cats and also helps keep hair balls (which result from any cat's self-grooming) from forming in any cat's stomach.

Regular grooming by a human is also an ideal way to keep track of a cat's general state of health. Lusterless fur, scaly or flaky skin, bald patches, fleas, and other signs of possible health problems can be detected by an observant groomer.

And perhaps equally important, grooming can be enjoyable for both cat and human. A cat loves to be stroked and will purr almost immediately upon being touched gently. Grooming is an important way in which cats communicate with each other and one of the best ways for humans to communicate with their cats.

A kitten may take a while to adjust to grooming (belly fur is particularly sensitive). Long-haired cats won't like it if their fur is pulled hard, so it may take a couple of sessions to develop the right touch.

Cats with short hair need to be groomed only occasionally, perhaps once a week. Brush short-haired cats in the direction of the grain, using quick, gentle strokes. Longhairs should have more frequent attention. Brush against the grain; then smooth the hair into place with a comb. Badly matted coats can be dealt with by cutting the mats out with blunt scissors pointed away from the skin. In really tough cases a vet's help may be needed because of the pain that can be involved in brushing or clipping out these matted areas.

A cat's coat may be his crowning glory, but it isn't the only part of the anatomy that requires care. When you make your regular once-over, take note of the condition of the eyes, ears, teeth, whiskers, and claws. If you get to know what these look like when they're healthy, you'll be in a good position to know when something is wrong and needs special attention.

Eyes don't need any particular care if they are clear and bright-looking, but if there is a mucous discharge, gently wipe off the accumulated matter with a piece of cotton soaked in warm water. If the eye seems red and irritated or if the third eyelid (cats have an extra membrane) covers part of the eyeball, your cat should be examined by a vet, who will recommend medication.

Ears are very sensitive and should be handled with great care. Never poke around inside the ears, but wipe the visible area of the ears clean with a piece of cotton to prevent the buildup of foreign matter, which can attract ear mites and infection. If anything looks irregular, ask the vet for help; don't attempt to treat the ear yourself.

Teeth should be clean, white, and complete (thirty in adult cats, twenty-six in kittens), but do not brush them or remove accumulated tartar yourself. Dry food or cat biscuits will help relieve a teething kitten (four to seven months old) and will keep tartar from building up in older cats. Decay, abscesses, broken or lost teeth should get a vet's attention. Any peculiar odor coming from the cat's mouth should be considered a sign of trouble.

Whiskers are extremely sensitive and should not be tampered with in any way. Some authorities believe that whiskers help cats determine whether a passageway will be wide enough to get through; others think that whiskers help prevent eye damage in underbrush or in fights. We don't know, but you might be interested to note that when you touch a cat's whiskers, he will probably blink his eyes. *Never* trim or cut whiskers.

Toenails in cats are remarkable tools. Because cats need long claws for hunting, yet must walk quietly when they stalk, nature has provided them with

retractable claws. Cats who do not get sufficient nail exercise may have to be manicured from time to time, or they will manicure themselves by scratching things (preferably upholstery). Clipping cat claws is a fearful occupation to many people, who are frightened of cutting the blood vessel that runs down into each claw. When you clip, use a professional clipper, and cut only the translucent part of the nail, a little bit at a time if it makes you feel better. If you should cause bleeding, apply a styptic pencil to the end of the claw.

Cats traditionally hate water on their coats, and it's not surprising that they hate baths, too. But when a cat becomes horribly dirty or has gotten into an unpleasant substance that can't be removed with a brush or comb, a bath may be necessary. Dry shampoos are often effective when the problem is odor, but a full-fledged bath may be the only way to get a muddy cat clean. Cat shampoos are available commercially. Get someone to help you hold the cat, and use a sizable sink or tub where you can keep control. Water should be lukewarm or just about body temperature. Before washing the cat, put a bit of cotton in each ear and a drop of mineral oil in each eye for protection, and then rinse him in water. Apply the shampoo all over, avoiding the ears and eyes, scrub gently, and then rinse thoroughly. Although you will want to make the bath as brief as possible, don't skip over the rinsing part because residual soap can cause irritation. After rinsing, dry the cat thoroughly in a soft towel and keep him indoors and out of drafts until he has completely reverted to his usual fuzzy self. Don't use a hair dryer to dry his fur; his delicate skin may get burned, and it may terrify him. It may take an hour or more before he'll forgive you, but that's just one of the difficult moments in life you must learn to accept.

Declawing

Declawing is a controversial issue. Many cat people feel that declawing is cruel and unnatural because it involves surgery and deprives the cat of his natural defenses against other animals.

Those who have their cats declawed generally do so to protect their furniture against their cats' scratches. Cats can usually be trained to use a scratching post and keep their claws off the furniture. But if you've made repeated attempts at scratching-post training and still have a scratch-happy cat, you'll have to weigh the facts on declawing for yourself.

Declawing should be done only by a veterinarian, who removes the entire roots of the toenails on the front paws. The process is irreversible—the claws won't grow back. The cat's feet will be sore for a few days, and the process can be painful, especially for older cats. Once the feet have healed, the cat can walk normally, but generally he shouldn't be allowed outside since he no longer has his claws for protection.

Medical Matters

One of the most important things to do when you first get your cat is to line up a veterinarian. If possible, find out from the cat's original owner who the vet has been and what shots the cat has had. Or call a vet in the neighborhood (on the recommendation of a friend, the local humane shelter, or the local chapter of the Veterinary Medical Association, or check the Yellow Pages), and make an appointment for the earliest possible time. A kitten must be inoculated against distemper at six to eight weeks of age, but every new cat deserves an early examination regardless of age.

For the first visits to the vet and any subsequent ones, don't feed the cat for several hours beforehand, and if possible, keep him confined until you are ready to leave. Many cats can sense that a visit to the vet is in the offing and will make themselves scarce. Check the litter box for a piece of stool, and wrap it in a plastic wrap or bag to take along so the vet can examine it for parasites.* Transport your nervous patient in his carrier, and reassure him constantly with your voice. It's a good idea to keep a record of your cat's medical visits and to make note of when he's set for another trip to the vet so no important shots will be missed.

"An ounce of prevention is worth a pound of cure," goes the old saying, and it certainly is true for cats. Don't think of the vet as just an emergency measure for a serious accident or illness. Taking your cat for an annual checkup is a way to keep your cat in good health.

Don't try to diagnose ailments yourself, but become familiar with the common symptoms, methods of first aid, and home treatment. And keep your vet's name and telephone number within easy reach and on hand for yourself and any cat-sitters.

* Once again, pregnant women should avoid handling cat feces because of the danger of toxoplasmosis.

Here are some symptoms to watch out for:

Sudden weight loss
Frequent vomiting
Refusal to eat for twenty-four hours
Persistent diarrhea or constipation for more than a day
Runny eyes and nose; sneezing
Constant scratching
Peculiar behavior, such as crying, loss of balance, listlessness, unusually bad temper

Some of these symptoms may, in fact, indicate serious illness. Others may be signs of trouble that can quickly be cured, either in the vet's office or at home under a vet's guidance.

HOW TO TREAT A VETERINARIAN

Most people think that vets treat cats. Wrong, or at least not entirely true. Any cat must learn how to treat vets, or the whole experience of a visit to the vet can be a disaster. Here are some useful bits of advice.

You will know that you are about to go to the vet's office when your human starts acting awfully nice although he's done nothing wrong, like lose your catnip toy. Out comes the cat carrier, and before you know it, in you go. Practice preventive medicine (meaning how to prevent getting medicine, of course). Do not express curiosity about the carrying case. If you can't hide, get up on the highest piece of furniture in the room. Stay there, and pretend to be asleep.

If you lose the battle, do not lose the war. Once you arrive at the vet's office, be so quiet in your case that your human will get curious and open the top. When he does, run for your life.

If that fails, tough it out. Don't meow; don't hiss or fuzz up. Just stand there on the exam table, and act cool. But when the vet touches you, yowl as loud as you know how. If nothing else, everyone in the waiting room will think that you are being abused and will file out quietly. You haven't saved yourself, but all those other cats out there will be forever grateful.

If the vet attempts to give you a pill, don't protest, but don't swallow it either. Just hold it on the back of your tongue, and when the vet turns around to write stuff on your card, spit the pill politely into your handkerchief.

When the needle gets near your nether end, fuzz up as much as possible. The vet may miss.

If you've been unsuccessful in your treatment of the vet, don't mope. Just make sure that they spell your name right on the card.

First Aid

Accidents can happen, in spite of your precautions, and knowing how to handle an injured cat properly can mean the difference between life and death. If an accident occurs and your cat seems seriously injured, call the veterinarian immediately. He will advise you if your cat needs to be brought in for treatment and of any steps you should take. This chart outlines some important emergency and other health measures cat owners should be familiar with.

Moving an Injured Cat	If the cat is hysterical or impossible to handle, wrap him in a towel or blanket, keeping a firm hold. Transport the cat to car in blanket. Hold the cat gently but firmly until you reach the vet's. If you cannot hold the cat, place him carefully in carrier.
Bleeding	If bleeding is profuse, apply a pressure bandage—any soft clean cloth applied firmly and directly over the wound until bleeding stops. If blood is spurting rapidly and pressure bandage does not work, use a tourniquet; tie a piece of cloth loosely around joint above wound, and tighten until blood stops flowing. Keep it tied tightly one or two minutes; then loosen slightly. If blood is still flowing, repeat, but try to get to the vet as quickly as possible.
Broken Bones	Handle the cat with great care, and get to the vet immediately for treatment.

Shock	Keep the cat warm in a blanket or cat carrier, and get to the vet right away.
Bite Wounds	Wash gently with a mild saline solution, but do not attempt to treat the wound yourself, except to control bleeding. Without proper treatment, puncture wounds will quickly become infected and cause abscesses.
Insect Stings	Clean the area. If swelling occurs, apply ice; watch carefully for any change in behavior, vomiting, or shock. If any signs develop, call the vet immediately.
Poisoning	Poisoned cats may vomit, cry, whimper, breathe heavily, stagger, convulse, have abdominal pain. Determine the source of poisoning, if possible, and call the vet immediately.
Choking	Attempt to dislodge the substance causing choking; compress the cat's abdomen quickly just behind rib cage. If the cat is unconscious, you may try to remove object by carefully inserting spoon or eraser end of pencil into his throat.
Burns	Apply ice or cold water immediately to the burned area for about a minute. Unless burn is minor and heals quickly, call the vet.
Cystitis	A common bladder infection; it causes pain when the cat urinates and can lead to death if untreated. Symptoms are squatting in the litter box and straining on urinating, especially by male cats. Your vet will prescribe appropriate medication.
Administering Medicine	Never give your cat a pill or any medication without checking first with the vet. Ask your vet to demonstrate the proper method for giving your cat medication.

Preventive Medicine

Thanks to modern veterinary research, many diseases that were once fatal to cats can now be controlled, and serious illness can often be avoided altogether by having your cat inoculated with the various vaccines that are now available, as recommended by your vet.

Very young kittens are usually protected against viruses because of the antibodies in their mothers' milk, but after the weaning period, it is up to the owner to provide protection. This kind of preventive medicine need not be expensive—indeed, it is far less costly than treating disease—nor need it be troublesome in terms of effort.

Common cat diseases for which vaccines are available are rabies, feline distemper, and feline respiratory diseases (these are numerous, but vaccines exist for three of them: rhinotracheitis, calcivirus, and pneumonitis).* Most vaccines are given on an annual basis during the yearly checkup. Your vet will undoubtedly keep a record of your cat's inoculations and send you a reminder notice when boosters are due, but it's always a good idea to keep your own records as well. Don't assume that your cat is immune to disease because he never comes into contact with other animals; some viruses can be carried on clothing, and some diseases are transmitted by insects or mice, rather than by direct contact with another cat.

Vaccines do vary in type and application, so be sure to discuss timing and possible aftereffects with your vet—starting with that first important visit to the vet when your cat arrives in your household or at weaning time if you are raising kittens yourself. If you plan to take your cat to a boarding kennel or a show, you should take the precaution of having your vet examine him a week before you go.

Parasites

Internal parasites or worms are extremely common in cats, particularly in kittens. When you make your regular visit to the vet, remember to take along a stool sample from your cat so the vet can examine it for the presence of parasites and prescribe appropriate treatment, if needed.

It is always discomfiting, to say the least, to discover that you've been keeping not just one animal—your lovely cat—but several, in the form of fleas, ticks, or other such creeps, collectively known as external parasites, who've been using your cat for a free ride. There are a number of commercial prepa-

* One particularly serious disease, almost always fatal, is feline leukemia, for which there is no preventive inoculation. A great deal of research is now being done on this puzzling disease, and it is hoped that prevention will eventually become possible. It is not known exactly how the disease is transmitted, but it can be diagnosed by a blood test, and any early sign of symptoms (any of the symptoms listed on page 59 may be indicators of feline leukemia) should alert the owner to see the vet without delay.

rations on the market for these pests, but we recommend that you ask your vet to suggest remedies rather than try to cure the problem on your own. Many home cures are not very effective, and some can even be harmful.

Study this table so you'll know if your cat is being invaded and what to do about it.

INTERNAL PARASITES

Roundworms	Signs, if any, are loss of weight, digestive upset. Very common. Can be serious in adult cats, fatal in kittens. Can be contagious to humans, causing serious problems.
Hookworms	Severe intestinal problems, can cause anemia, possibly death. Common in warm climates. One sign is bloody stools. Transmission to humans is possible but rare.
Tapeworms	Signs, if any, are tapeworm segments in cat's stool, weight loss, scruffy coat, abdominal distension (enlarged stomach). Also somewhat transmissible to humans.

EXTERNAL PARASITES

Fleas	The most common external parasite. Bloodsuckers that irritate the skin around the head, neck, and tail, often causing severe dermatitis if not controlled. They may also infest your house and transmit other parasites, such as tapeworms. Serious infestations warrant a vet's attention. Fleas are contagious to humans.
Ticks	Common particularly in warm climates. Ticks bury their heads in the cat's skin. To remove, don't pull, or the tick's head may remain. Remove by rubbing the tick with bits of cotton soaked in alcohol until it lets go. Flush or burn the tick. If the infestation is serious, consult your vet. Humans can be hosts to ticks, too.
Lice	Cause excessive scratching. Can be serious, so ask the vet for advice.
Mites	Mites usually attack the cat's ear canal. To prevent this, keep the cat's ears clean of dirt or wax. If cat shakes his head constantly,

	scratches his ears, or rubs his head, mites may be the cause. See the vet for treatment.
Ringworms	Signs are hair loss around ears, face, tail, legs, bald patches, raw skin, and scabs, but ringworm cannot be diagnosed without special testing and examination by a vet. Since the organism causing ringworm also affects humans and since cat hair can provide a source of infection for more than a year on the premises, a vet's attention is necessary; medications are available.

The Aging Cat

Although a cat's normal life span is about twelve years, many indoor cats that get good care will live up to twenty years. Good care includes a sound nutritional program (no overfeeding, please, since obesity will inevitably shorten life) and good preventive medical attention from you and your veterinarian—be sure to take your cat in for his annual checkups.

It is not always easy to tell when a cat reaches his twilight years, but he will gradually become less active and may lose some sight or hearing as the fur around his mouth begins to whiten with age. Teeth may be affected as gums recede, and you should keep an alert eye out for missing teeth and gum infections. Soften the cat's food in water or mash it into a pudding consistency to aid in digestion, and watch the quantity of water that the cat drinks. A heavy intake of water—or very little—may indicate some kidney problems, and difficulty in urinating or eliminating may call for a check with the vet.

Some people feel that the best "cure" for old age is the introduction of a new kitten into the household—and for some cats this may be true. But many older cats take any change in routine very hard. Don't insist on playtime or expect regular attendance at the supper dish if the cat seems to prefer sleeping to anything else. If your cat doesn't turn up for meals, however, you might try to encourage an extra feeding here and there, so long as you don't overdo the amount. When a cat loses hearing or eyesight, he may also lose a sense of time, and it will be up to you to remind him when dinner is ready. Keep an eye out for unusual behavior that may signal some disorder. But generally there won't be anything special to do for your older cat, except to give him extra doses of affection.

8
The Traveling Cat

Or, letting the rest of the world know you're a superstar

Even if you're not a globe-trotter yourself, your cat will have to make a trip every once in a while—even if it's only an annual visit to the vet. But many a cat gets the chance to do a great deal more than that: spending weekends or vacations away, going to boarding kennels, or—like Morris during his busy season—virtually living out of a catcase in the role of superstar. Some cats love to travel; some hate it; others may tolerate it because they'd rather be with their humans than alone at home. Whatever the attitude of your own cat and whatever your own travel habits, you should always be prepared for the contingency. This doesn't mean that you'll need a matched set of Vuitton luggage for your puss (though it wouldn't be entirely inappropriate), but you should have on hand a sturdy carrier (as discussed on page 29) just in case.

Convincing your cat that this is an essential piece of equipment may not be easy. A day or two before a trip, bring the carrying case out, and let the cat familiarize himself with its interior. To entice him, line the bottom of the case with a soft cloth or shredded newspaper, and sprinkle some dry food inside. Keep the lid open, and let the cat explore to his heart's content. When you are ready to go, encourage the cat to jump in, and gently but quickly close the lid. Do not shout "AHA!" Say "Nice kitty" in a soothing tone of voice, and keep up the reassuring chitchat as you carry him away. If possible, stay within hearing distance of the case so the cat can hear you as long as he is inside. Do not open the carrier again until you are safely in an enclosed room despite your

Learning to pack properly is only one of the tricks the traveling cat must master. The first step is to be sure you get packed yourself.

cat's yowls or any mysterious silence. Most cats will take advantage of an opened lid to head for the hills, and if you are in unfamiliar territory, they may easily become lost. Even in an automobile, keep the carrier shut; it's obviously unsafe to be driving along the highway with a cat clinging to your shoulder or trying to curl up under the accelerator. Never let the carrier stand in direct sunshine or in any spot that is not well ventilated.

If you are able to train your cat to a leash, you may find this a more convenient and pleasurable mode of transport than a cat carrier. In any case (or without a case), don't try to carry your cat in your arms without some restraining measure if you hope to see him again.

Leash training is not easy with an adult cat, but if yours is still young and impressionable, you can give it a try. First, get the kitten to wear a collar for a few days until he doesn't pay any attention to it; then attach a string about two feet long to the collar, and let the kitten drag it around the house. Play with the kitten by holding the string and calling his name as you tug him toward you. When this works, attach a heavier leather leash to the collar. Repeat the procedure until the cat follows you when you call his name. It may take a while before the cat will behave on the leash outdoors, but continue to call and tug, reassuring and praising him when he does what you want.

Taking a Trip

For a short trip by car, don't feed the cat for a couple of hours before you leave, and wait until you are back home before offering water or food. Some cats will vomit because of carsickness (experienced car travelers will usually be fine) or may even eliminate right in the carrier, causing unpleasantness for everyone concerned, especially himself. Clean up the mess in the box as soon as you have the opportunity, and be sure to remove the odor, which would remind the cat to do the same thing the next time out.

If you must leave the cat alone in the car during the trip, do not leave the windows of the car shut, especially if the weather is warm. The internal temperature of an automobile increases alarmingly if all the windows are closed, and cats have been known to die of heatstroke or suffocation even on temperate days.

When planning a long trip by car, do not expect that every motel or hotel you visit will accept your feline friend with open arms. Check ahead, and reassure the management that you will leave no signs of the cat when you check out. Along the way, stop every few hours to give the cat a chance to drink some water, but don't feed him until you have arrived at your destination for the evening. Have with you in the car a familiar kitty-litter pan and food and water dishes from home. Anything familiar will help your cat tolerate the trip.

If you plan to travel by train, plane, or ship and take your cat along, there are some things you should investigate before you take off.

Find out whether there are any special regulations for cat passengers: if your cat can travel in passenger sections (generally allowed in planes, but in very limited numbers; not usually permitted in trains) or if he must go in the baggage compartment. If your cat must travel in the baggage section, make sure you're comfortable with these accommodations—people often worry that compartments may become too hot or cold for their pets.

Find out if there are any specific requirements for cat carriers, as to size, etc. Using a carrier with a rounded top, incidentally, will lessen the chance of your prized package's being stacked with other baggage. Be sure to identify the carrier properly with your name, home address, telephone number, and lots of words in large print like "Caution: Live Animal," "Cat," and "This Side Up" as well as whatever else officials request.

If you're making a connecting flight, find out if you will be able to check on your cat during the interval.

Look into interstate or international regulations regarding transport of cats. Officials generally require a health certificate of some sort, and there may be other regulations, such as quarantine.

If your cat is to be shipped unaccompanied, it's a good idea to call an animal agency specializing in animal transport which will make arrangements for feeding, pickup, and delivery, etc.

TRAVELING IN STYLE

Needless to say, I have spent a good part of my life on the road—first on the street but eventually on the road, from the Great White Way to Sunset Boulevard, and a lot of pretty fancy avenues in between. I've been around, and I can tell you that, east or west, the castle is best. Nevertheless, I have learned to cope with my nomadic life-style, and I have picked up a few tidbits of wisdom along the way.

You will know when your human is planning a trip because he will suddenly plant a suitcase on the bed and start filling it. As soon as the underwear goes in, jump into the suitcase, and curl up, looking absolutely adorable. It won't always work, but the human will always feel a real twinge of guilt as he finishes preparing for the trip. Besides, it's a good place for a catnap, however brief.

If your human should travel without you, leaving you alone overnight, there's plenty of stuff you can do to amuse yourself. The old toilet-paper trick is always a good one, but you can try several other ploys. When the cat-sitter comes to feed you, hide in the closet, and don't come out, no matter what. Make the sitter think you have disappeared. It's not nice, but it will make everyone think twice about leaving you again.

When your human returns after such a trip, don't welcome him back with wide-open arms. Don't purr. If you can manage it, don't even acknowledge his return. Give him an hour or so of the cold shoulder, and then act friendly, as if you had just noticed his presence.

When you hear the telltale rattle of the carrier being taken down from the shelf, do not spend even a minute wondering whether it's Bermuda this time or just a day trip to the beach. Head for the linen closet or under the guest room bed (not, repeat not, *to one of your usual haunts), and be terribly quiet. It is hard to keep this up past dinnertime, but by then your human will have missed the train or that appointment at the vet's.*

Boy, do they have a lot to learn! Stick around, kids, I've got a lot to teach.

9
The Facts of Life

Or, how to teach humans that birds and bees have nothing to do with real life in a book about cats

One of the most important facts of life to be faced by the cat person is sex. Although kittens are too young to have much in the way of sex characteristics, unneutered cats most definitely do acquire sexual natures as they mature, something that happens quite quickly, within the first year. Tomcats tend to roam in search of females, fight other toms, and spray foul-smelling urine around the house to show everyone just whose furniture it really is.* Unspayed female cats usually go into heat twice a year (for a period of several weeks, going in and out of heat for a few days at a time) and can drive many a human up the wall with their rolling, crying, and frustration if they do not have a male around to satisfy the urge to breed. Female cats in heat who are allowed outside the house invariably turn up pregnant, and finding homes for kittens you can't care for is not an easy job.

To Neuter or Not to

The overpopulation of cats is a serious problem these days, and altogether too many of them end up in humane shelters or pounds without any hope for the future. Conscientious cat people, therefore, generally opt to have their cats neutered at the first opportunity, usually at about six months, before

* Altered cats, especially those kept with other cats, may still spray in the house away from the litter box, but this is a natural territorial behavior probably caused by competition, and the odor is not nearly so rank as that produced by a tomcat.

the onset of sexual maturity. Not only does this procedure make a better pet—a cat less likely to roam, fight, or get lost—but it also keeps the cat population under control and your house somewhat more pleasant-smelling. It may even make the cat's life a bit longer. Spayed female cats are less susceptible to mammary tumors, and altered male cats are less prone to abscesses caused by bite wounds or to the dangers of getting lost or killed while roaming.

A number of cat people avoid dealing with the issue of altering or spaying because they think it is expensive; fattening for the cat; or cruel and unnatural in depriving the animal of pleasure. As for expense, neutering is surgery performed by a veterinarian, so you're paying for a professional service. If the prices quoted by your veterinarian seem too high for you, check with your local humane shelter to see if there is a spay-neuter clinic in your vicinity. As for the second argument, neutering is not the cause of obesity, but overfeeding an underexercised cat is. And the deprivation argument has nothing to do with cruelty. Most cats neutered before maturity never know what they are missing, and surely it is more cruel to allow a cat to become injured in a fight over a female or to bring unwanted kittens into the world.

Besides, as Morris points out, some aspects of the sex game can have expensive legal consequences. There was a time, we are told, when Morris—who always has an eye for an attractive feminine feline—found himself the focus of a number of threats of paternity suits. When questioned on the subject, Morris simply clams up and points to his lawyer, but we're pretty sure that it was his loose pre-superstar life as a tom that got him into these predicaments.

Growing Your Own

Sometimes kitten raising is inevitable; mostly, though, it is only considered a truly desirable circumstance by professional cat breeders who want kittens to show or sell. When a female cat comes home in the family way, as she always will if given the chance, you will probably not even notice that she is pregnant until a week or two before delivery. A vet can usually determine pregnancy at about twenty-five to thirty days after conception; pregnancy lasts about fifty-eight to sixty-four days.

Except for adding some dry milk and calcium supplements to the new mother's diet, there is not a great deal for you to do until kittening time approaches. Then you can busy yourself by preparing a kittening box—a cardboard carton about two feet by two feet with six-inch-high sides, lined with a soft towel and placed in a relatively dark, draft-free, out-of-the-way corner, will make a perfectly suitable place for your cat to give birth. Be sure to encourage your cat to explore this bed beforehand, however, for chances are that she will choose to have her kittens someplace totally inappropriate if she doesn't know that is what you've done all the fussing for. I've known mother cats to choose closets, laundry baskets, and even their humans' beds.

Actual delivery of the first kitten should take place within an hour after the onset of labor. You will know that your cat is in labor when her breathing becomes faster (she may even pant) and when she starts moving her legs in a rhythmic motion. As soon as a kitten is born, wrapped in his protective amniotic sac, the mother should begin immediately to remove the sac, break the umbilical cord with her teeth, and lick the kitten all over to clean and dry him. If she does not attend to these matters, you can pierce the bag yourself (using only your fingers, please) and clean the kitten in a soft piece of toweling. Tie some sterile string around the umbilical cord two inches from the kitten's abdomen, and then cut the cord on the side toward the mother with blunt sterile scissors. (String and scissors can be made sterile by being boiled for ten minutes in water.) If the mother fails to clean her kittens, use the toweling to rub the kitten yourself until he makes a cry and seems eager to nurse.

Cat litters usually range in number from two to eight. The whole birth procedure can take as long as six or seven hours, during which time you should be observant, but otherwise, leave well enough alone unless the mother ignores a kitten or seems to be having trouble delivering the next one, in which case you should call the vet. After the last one is born, the mother will relax her body, and her abdomen will become flaccid and deflated.

Within three or four hours of delivery, you should change the top layer of lining in the box, but otherwise, leave the kittens alone. Keep water in a bowl near the box since the mother may well be thirsty and be sure to offer her food. She will, over the next three or four weeks, have an enormous appetite, but keep her supplied with as much food as she wants; she is, after all, supporting a family.

The day after delivery, it might be a good idea to take the mother cat to the vet for a checkup, if she seems particularly weak, and perhaps the kittens, too, if one or more of them appears to be noticeably smaller or weaker than the others. Put the mother cat in her carrier, and keep the kittens in their box, securely and warmly wrapped in a blanket.

At about ten days, the kittens' eyes should open. If any one seems to have difficulty, moisten a cotton swab, and wipe the eyes gently. Because their eyes will be sensitive at first, make certain that the kittens stay in a relatively dark area until they are perhaps three weeks old. By this time they will be full of energy and inquisitiveness, scrambling about, walking, and getting out of the nursery box. The mother should now begin to toilet train them to the litter box.

Also at the age of about three weeks, the kittens will begin showing a taste for solid food, and you should begin offering it to them. By four weeks they will display a real preference for it, and you should increase the amount in their diet, feeding them soft cat food four times a day. As they reach the age of five weeks, reduce the number of meals to three a day, making certain that each kitten gets about one ounce of food per pound of body weight every day. By the time the kittens are completely weaned, at about six weeks, you may reduce their meals to two a day, but many cat people feel that the three-meal-a-day schedule should continue until the kittens are a few months old.

When the kittens are six weeks old, it is time to make that crucial visit to the vet for their first inoculations.

While you are at the vet's, you might inform him that you will soon be having kittens available for good homes if all are somehow not already accounted for—thoughtful cat people won't let their cats breed without lining up homes for the kittens ahead of time.

There are a number of ways to find suitable homes, but some are more satisfactory than others. Friends who want kittens are the best, of course, because you'll be able to check up on their progress. Sometimes friends will be able to make matches for you, and you will find that veterinarians may help place a kitten with a client who wants a second cat or has recently lost one. Advertising through local newspapers can often bring results, although I would recommend that you carefully check out any responders to the ad—either by sizing them up when they come to call on the kittens or by checking out the potential home.

The Last Word

The Morris Approach. It's so simple and effective that any human can be trained to follow it. (I've even known humans who were taught to open a cat food can at the sound of a meow.) If you wonder whether you have mastered the Approach, your cat will be glad to let you know if you have missed a point or two. Look for messages outside his litter box. Or for notes scratched on your furniture. If you're having problems, brush up on some of the chapters in this book. Or brush your cat. Or open a can of 9-Lives, and talk about it over tuna. Spend a few moments doing something you both enjoy . . . like watching one of my commercials.

As a superstar, I am loved by millions, but most cats are content to be loved by just one or two and will wait for you to come around. After all, your cat knows you're only human.

All the comforts of home and only a few hours until breakfast. What more could a finicky cat want?

Common Breeds

The following descriptions of some of the established cat breeds illustrate the impressive lengths to which professional breeders have gone in perfecting our species. Of course, my own preference is for the homegrown variety of cat—in particular the Orange Domestic Short Hair—even though cat-breed associations haven't accorded us any special distinction. True cat lovers, though, don't attach much importance to family trees, but take their cats as they find them, long- or short-haired and in any color of the rainbow.

Abyssinian A short-haired cat with a slender muscular body and legs, a tapering tail with a black tip, and pointed ears. There are two color types: a rich tawny-copper Aby and the Red Abyssinian, considered a separate breed in England, which is probably where the basic Abyssinian breed originated. A lively cat with a great curiosity.

Birman The sacred cat of Burma and an increasingly popular breed of long-haired cats. The body is golden yellow, and the face, ears, and tail are deep brown; but the paws are pure white. Legs are short and strong, the tail is bushy and medium in length, and the face is wide with full cheeks. Eyes are sapphire blue.

British Blue, Black, and Brown Three breeds of short-haired cats with dense coats and very sociable, mild-mannered personalities. Eyes are yellow or orange, and the coats must not have a trace of tabby marking or any color other than the basic one.

Burmese A cat who hails not from Burma, but from America, where it was developed in 1936. Most Burmese are deep brown in color, but there are several color varieties (chocolate, lilac, cream, etc.). The coat is short, the body is long and lithe, and the eyes are slanty and yellow. Friendly like the Siamese, the Burmese is less vocal and a bit less highly strung.

Chinchilla An elegant white long-haired cat, originated in England during the 1880s. The undercoat is white, but the black or silver tips on the long hairs give a silvery appearance. The kittens are born with tabby rings on their tails. This cat looks very delicate but is actually extremely tough and needs no particular coddling except for grooming.

Himalayan A long-haired American breed, the result of a cross between the Persian and the Siamese, which is exactly what the cat looks like, with a basic beige body coat and deep seal brown points. The eyes are large and blue, and the body tends to be large and broad. Not as talkative as the Siamese, this cat is very affectionate and pleasant to be around.

Maine Coon Cat Probably a cross between a long-haired breed and a domestic tabby shorthair, this remarkable American breed is a striking, large, and generally impressive animal. The Maine Coon Cat seems to love to climb (like the raccoon), and though it has longish hair, it doesn't require the constant grooming of a Persian.

Manx Originated on the Isle of Man, this tailless short-haired cat is the result of selective breeding to develop what was once a mutant characteristic. The hind legs are longer than the forelegs, and the gait is strange and bobbing; the cat doesn't seem to miss having a tail, for its balance nonetheless is good and its speed is swift. Inquisitive and faithful, the Manx is also independent and can show an irritable temper occasionally.

Persian The most popular long-haired breed, it comes in a variety of colors. The origin is uncertain; it may come from Persia, and it may not; but it's been a well-established breed for years. Those with blue eyes are most likely born deaf, but the orange-eyed Persians are fine, as are those with one orange eye and one blue eye. The head is very big, the face very wide, and the overall effect very impressive.

Rex This is not a breed so much as a curly-coated type or mutation that will show up in various breeds. There are what are considered two distinct Rex breeds in England and others in other countries. The body tends to be slender with long legs. The short, wavy hair does not shed.

Russian Blue

Although this cat is not blue, but gray, it really is from Russia. (There is also an American Blue, based on the Russian breed.) A short-haired cat with a graceful body, long legs and tail, and green, almond-shaped eyes, this cat is beautiful and extremely gentle. It is shy and unassertive, and many people feel that it makes a perfect companion for a city-dwelling human since it is both affectionate and takes well to apartment life.

Siamese

One of the most popular short-haired breeds, the Siamese may not actually be from Siam, but it does have Oriental origins. The coat is basically light cream or beige with ears, mask, paws, and tail of another color, most commonly seal brown (though there are now several color varieties including blue, lilac, tortoiseshell, red, chocolate, and tabby). The Siamese is intelligent, affectionate, extremely vocal, and very energetic considering its slender build. The eyes are always blue, and the face should be wedge-shaped with a fine muzzle.

Further Reading

Although I have tried to get all of my hard-won knowledge into this book, I'll have to admit that I couldn't cover everything—if only because my experience, though vast, hasn't been all-encompassing. (I've never given birth to kittens, for instance, or spent much time around a vet's office, or been Siamese.) Therefore, I want to include the names of some additional useful books for the literary-minded to peruse once they have become owned by a cat.

Browder, Sue. *The Pet Name Book.* New York: Workman Publishing Co., Inc., 1979.
For those who need inspiration.

Fireman, Judy, editor. *The Cat Catalog.* New York: Workman Publishing Co., Inc., 1976.
For those who love to browse in books devoted entirely to the most superior of species.

Fox, Michael W. *Understanding Your Cat.* New York: Coward, McCann & Geoghegan, Inc., 1974.
No human can fully understand a cat, but this veterinarian-cum-psychologist comes pretty close.

Gebhardt, Richard H., editor. *A Standard Guide to Cat Breeds.* New York: McGraw-Hill, 1979.
Everything you want to know and more about this subject.

Gerstenfeld, Sheldon L., V.M.D. *Taking Care of Your Cat: A Complete Guide to Your Cat's Medical Care.* Reading, Mass.: Addison-Wesley Publishing Co., Inc., 1979.
McGinnis, Terri. *The Well Cat Book.* New York: Random House, Inc., 1975.
Both of these will make useful additions to the human's medicine chest.